FEELING UNUSUAL

PREVIOUS BOOKS BY ANN DRYSDALE

Poetry Books
The Turn of the Cucumber, 1995, Peterloo Poets
Gay Science, 1999, Peterloo Poets
Backwork, 2002, Peterloo Poets
Between Dryden and Duffy: Another Collection, 2005, Peterloo Poets
Quaintness and Other Offences, 2009, Cinnamon Press
Turn, 2013, Exot Books
Miss Jekyll's Gardening Boots, 2015, Shoestring Press
Vanitas, 2019, Shoestring Press

Other Books
Faint Heart Never Kissed a Pig, 1982, Routledge and Kegan Paul
Sows' Ears and Silk Purses, 1984, Routledge and Kegan Paul
Pearls Before Swine, 1985, Routledge and Kegan Paul
A Pig in a Passage, 1997, Robert Hale
Real Newport, 2006, Seren
Three-three, two-two, five-six, 2007, Cinnamon Press
Discussing Wittgenstein, 2009, Cinnamon Press

FEELING UNUSUAL

ANN DRYSDALE

All rights reserved. No part of this work covered by the copyright herein may be reproduced or used in any means – graphic, electronic, or mechanical, including copying, recording, taping, or information storage and retrieval systems – without written permission of the publisher.

Printed by imprintdigital
Upton Pyne, Exeter
www.digital.imprint.co.uk

Typesetting and cover design by The Book Typesetters
us@thebooktypesetters.com
07422 598 168
www.thebooktypesetters.com

Published by Shoestring Press
19 Devonshire Avenue, Beeston, Nottingham, NG9 1BS
(0115) 925 1827
www.shoestringpress.co.uk

First published 2022
© Copyright: Ann Drysdale
© Cover painting: "The Mari Lwyd Brings Them Home Again" by Allison Neal
© Author photograph by Derek Adams

The moral right of the author has been asserted.

ISBN 978-1-912524-98-3

ACKNOWLEDGEMENTS

Thanks are due to the editors of journals in which some of these poems have appeared, including Acumen, The Oldie, The Spectator, Better Than Starbucks, New Verse News, Potcake Chapbooks and several anthologies from Grey Hen Press. Some formed part of a multi-media exhibition, "Track and Trace", and *Tench* was a winner in the 2019 Buzzwords competition.

I am grateful to Allison Neal for permission to use her painting on the cover and to Frank Olding for his translation of the poem on page 22.

Finally, a tip of my hat to the Mari Lwyd, the traditional hobbyhorse with a real skull, who goes about South Wales in the dark half of the year, taking part in mingled ceremonies of wassail and misrule. She entered my bailiwick as a passing interest and stayed on in the capacity of imaginary friend.

For those who give me ideas and trust me not to break them.

CONTENTS

Mari Lwyd Dances	1
Setting Off	2
Blue	3
Boat	4
Soup	5
Halva	6
Mari Lwyd Calls on a Kindred Spirit	7
Sticks	8
Sommerreise	9
Bridge	10
The Battle	11
My House is Shouting	12
Bed	13
Drawing the Waters	14
Mari Lwyd Finds the Forgotten Horses	15
Life in Ten Lines	16
How Beautiful are the Feet…	17
Make Yourself At Home	18
Absolution	19
Two poems about Spam	20
Nettles	21
Mari Lwyd Mends the Horses of Matholwch	22
And in Welsh…	23
Bones	24
Road Works	25
Clearing the Decks	30
Stones with Sad Faces	31
The Pond in July.	32
Mari Lwyd and the Postal Palaver	33
Black Cat Sinning	34
Fomite	35
Synchronicity	36
Prisoner	37
Quarterstaff	38
Fencing	39
Mission Impossible	40

Mari Lwyd with Bells and Whistles	41
Ballistic	42
Grown from a Stone	43
Nativity Play	44
Reclaiming the Abandoned Garden	45
Toad	48
Upon a Snail	49
Kiftsgate	50
Mari Lwyd will be Coming Soon	51
Seat	52
Badge of Honour	53
The Gravedigger Digs the Difference	54
Mari Lwyd meets Marie Lloyd.	55

MARI LWYD DANCES

Bone white, star bright
I have come to you tonight
I bear no malice, bring no sin
Open the door and let me in

    I am the horse that used to be
    the pitman's drudge or the punter's chance
    but benevolent death has set me free
    and off I go on my crazy dance.

    I shall dance that dance from dusk till dawn
    with the moon above and the road beneath.
    Having no hooves to drum my tune
    I'll dance to the clatter of my teeth.

    My worldly goods are few indeed;
    two worn-out boots and a gunny-sack
    though these are the only things I need
    to dance to the edge of the world and back.

    But the dance is fast and the road is long
    and sometimes I need to catch my breath
    so I stop at your door and I sing my song
    of the old illusions of life and death.

    I'll sing it for you and then I'll knock:
    Here I am, O my next of kin –
    and you will turn the key in the lock
    to keep me out or bring me in.

What you'll give I'll always take
Drink your beer and eat your cake
Where I am bound I do not know
Open the door and let me go

SETTING OFF

Pointed towards outdoors and set to go,
I cock my leg stiffly over the saddle
and settle my behind roughly amidships.

Feel for the pedals, slowly set them going
then, posting to a non-existent trot,
I build the rhythm to a steady hum.

Now I am heading straight across the road
and through the closed gate into the garden
where small birds feed unfazed. I pass unseen.

Brushing the ash tree with my right shoulder
I hurtle on, skimming the three stone steps
that lead into the little wilderness.

Having no brakes, I fly on through the brambles
where nature's creatures go about their business.
If I had wheels, I'd crash into the wall.

BLUE

It began with an interdental brush
at the foot of the stone steps to the terrace,
a tiny rectangle of brilliant blue.
Once spotted, I began to look for it
as I approached the corner where it was.
I felt the better for its being there
and glad to have it decorate my day.

And then it went. I searched at once in the
accumulated gubbins in the gutter,
fished with a stick under a few parked cars,
peered hopefully into the nearest drain.
I was surprised at how bereft I felt
when I was forced to face up to the fact
that it had gone, undoubtedly forever.

Later, as though by way of consolation,
other examples would appear at random,
dressed to impress in that peculiar blue;
a ball, a burst balloon, a bottle cap
crushed by a wheel into a crooked star.
These things are highlights in my Book of Hours
piercing the tired asphalt of the street
like precious touches of ultramarine
in mediaeval iconography.

BOAT

I open my own front door with my elbow;
in time of plague this is considered best.
Stepping direct from street to living room
I close it with a quick swing of my arse.
That's it. I'm in. Five-lever mortice lock
clicks into place to repel any boarders.
I know where I am now; I'm in a boat.
The narrow street outside is a towpath
and all the passers-by, a scant six feet
from where I watch them through my grubby portholes,
are either good folk out for exercise
or rough mechanicals about their business
and, while aboard, I shall remain in safety
until they, and the pestilence, have passed.

SOUP

Woman, gesticulating at the window
"Soup – you want soup?" She mimes a lifted elbow.
I must have looked aghast. "Soup" she repeats,
"we have soup in the car. Do you want some?"
I find a smile, hurriedly thrust it on
and send my answer through it. "No, thank you".

Three days into the lockdown, here they are
exhorted by the social media
to take good care of those who seem "at risk".
Kind folk intent on doing simple good
but I am left appalled to understand
I'm on their list of neighbours in decline.

Of course it's true; I am an old woman.
Three score and ten is the allotted span
and I'm already into extra time.
I'm looking back, but for the life of me
I can't determine at what point in it
I turned around and set a course for home.

HALVA

I love the way that it resists the knife
as the keen blade growls through the grittiness.
When I first lifted it from the posh box
it was a hefty wedge. Now bit by bit
it has become a roughly cubic block
and every time I slice a piece from it
I leave a little less. That's how it was
in childhood fields when the juddering combine
reduced the standing corn to a hearthrug
and village boys surrounded it with sticks
so as to kill and sell the fleeing rabbits.
The triumph and the sadness are the same
although the circumstances are less terrible.
No bloody cudgels reeking from the slaughter,
no broken bodies in triumphant hands,
just careful licking of the sticky knife
and the last piece of sweetness on my tongue.

MARI LWYD CALLS ON A KINDRED SPIRIT

I will knock on her door till she remembers
that she was once the Little Grey Pony,
whispering stories of her own adventures
into the busy silence of her head.
The door is already a little open;
if I knock softly I think she will hear.

She seldom spoke to adults in those days
since they worked to a separate agenda
that she had tried and failed to understand.
She never met their eyes but always listened
and almost always did as she was told
so as to let them know that she was there.

But at the times she felt herself alone,
she would make a wild mane of her cropped hair
to toss in time to her private whinnying
as she cantered, clattering in heavy shoes,
a leather satchel riding her recklessly
around the edges of the tarmac yard.

STICKS

That's how I'll spend the winter. In the shed
with the autumn harvest of possibles,
a greenhouse heater, an old yellow duster
and a new bottle of boiled linseed oil.

Taking the novices by their rough heads,
I'll run my closed hand down the lengths of them
to find the undesired excrescences
that spoil the feel of the eventual shaft.

Then out will come the old chip-carving tools,
the toenail clippers and the Stanley knife
to bring about the things I saw in them
when they were upside down in hedge and spinney.

There will be ferrules, fitted like new shoes,
firm rubber soles so that they tread safely
alongside needy feet. And quietly,
no Blind-Pew tapping to create unease.

I will keep at it till they're fit to serve
and with a pool of oil in my cupped cloth
I will anoint the smooth heads of the chosen
to bless them for the laying-on of hands.

SOMMERREISE

Riffing on an old poem, I repeat
a walk I used to do in better days;
the lower slopes of Blaina's spinal ridge.
Blundering down the ever-shifting scree,
I chunter cheerfully to a dead dog
in my hamfisted hendecasyllabics.
One small dog with a definite advantage,
four legs good and two manifestly less so…
I miss him. Now I go alone on three.

Sphinx-riddled, I continue my own journey
down old paths round the too-familiar
along with my lost dog and my last lover,
making their being dead and out of danger
into a curious kind of consolation.

BRIDGE

You mean well, but I wish you wouldn't say
that my dead dog has "crossed the Rainbow Bridge".
He's gone. It doesn't help to think of him
imprisoned somewhere else, where I can't reach him.

I'd rather have him nearer; in a place
where I can take him out and look at him
from time to time, along with what remains
of all his hairy peers. I call them up
like pulling out a necklace, bead by bead
from the warm depths of life's unlovely plughole.

Long ivory of the extended lurcher
spaced by dull days from border collie onyx.
Millefiore mongrels, colours shining
in celebration of their differences.

I coil them all together in my hand
revelling in their semi-preciousness
then wind the end around my middle finger
and let them all slide back into the dark
leaving my palm full of the smell of dog.

THE BATTLE
Between the Jesuits and the Franciscans

Bleary and one-eared in the early morning
I caught a name dropped from the purring radio
and held it for a moment in my head.
Ignatius of Loyola. An old friend
whose prayer I used to rattle off by heart.
How did it go again? I knew I knew
and called it with a languid fingersnap.

A quiet voice spake unto me at once,
"make me" it said "an instrument of thy peace".
"Where there is discord…" I replied. Then stopped.
This was the wrong voice and the wrong prayer,
parked like a cattletruck across the road
that led to the Society of Jesus.

"Oh, Francis of Assisi, go away
and take your prayer with you, I need to find
the one that I've mislaid. Saint Antony,
give me a clue. It's dark and I'm afraid."
But Francis stood his ground "where there is error…"

I tried to hold my nerve, telling myself
this was a new cross I must learn to bear
but that if I had faith, my memory
would pull the lost words like a string of flags
out of a prestidigitator's hat.

And as I breakfasted, Francis went out
to feed the birds with the last crumbs of toast.
Ignatius became Ignatz, chucked a brick
that made my head ring like a rattled bucket,
cried, "that'll teach you!" and it did indeed.
It served me right; it was what I deserved.

MY HOUSE IS SHOUTING

Half covered in leaves, none of them twitching
and not a soul in sight, my house is shouting.
Staccato calls, little halloos, sharp answers;
phatic communion of invisibles.

The ivy is alive; I feel it breathing
although the face of it is green and still.
Some spikes have extra berries; they are watching,
their unknown sum divisible by two.

As dusk descends to settle on the street
and curtained windows blossom one by one,
the cries coagulate, chip one another
into something that is almost music:

Move on, move on – there's nothing to see here.
No sparrows. Nope. What gave you that idea?

BED

This is my roost, my place of same-again.
Just as sparrows plug themselves one by one
into the ivy on the outer wall,
I part accumulated layers of
nocturnal comfort, sliding my worn self
into the waiting slot carved by long use
in old memory foam that can't forget
the one who comes like a devoted lover
night after night into its bailiwick.

This is the place that waits for me all day.
I am an old knife, carefully restored
to my allotted place in the canteen
and I will lie where I'm supposed to go
so that I know where I am to be found
next time I need to use myself again.

DRAWING THE WATERS
05.20hh GMT

Alan Kasujja, Nkem Ifejika,
wireless custodians of the hours of night,
news of the world; voices of Africa.

Now British diction interrupts the flow:
twenty past five, a greeting, a goodbye,
BBC Radio 4 is good to go.

News of sea areas, coastal stations, then
the iteration of the inshore waters.
My finger itches to explore again

and on the wrinkled counterpane I trace
the promontories of the land I love,
whisper anticipation of each place.

Cape Wrath to Rattray Head, familiar thrill,
Berwick to Whitby, following the coast,
Gibraltar Point, North Foreland, Selsey Bill.

Down and along. Lyme Regis to Land's End,
and then two heads, St David's and Great Orme,
each one announced like an expected friend.

Over to Ulster from the Isle of Man,
wave to the west from Ardnamurchan Point
and then I come to rest where I began.

When every lovely name has been and gone
my tracing-finger rests. All shall be well.
My home is whole; the day can carry on.

MARI LWYD FINDS THE FORGOTTEN HORSES

Her boots assume the consistency of bread
with hobnails softened into silent winegums.
Her mouth ajar so her teeth will not chatter
she takes a breath and tiptoes into limbo.

Here they spin, weightless, the aborted horses
in their various stages of completion,
each one imagined by an urban girl
and knitted bit by bit into existence.

They were the doors out of the ordinary
by way of books and toys and television.
Saddled with need and bridled with anxiety
they carried nervous passengers through puberty.

Some rode alone, others in Fives and Sevens;
all but a few dismounted when they felt
safe to proceed on foot, leaving their steeds
to fade into the shadows of new trees.

Here they remain, dreamed up and discarded,
some still unfinished, some beyond repair,
none of them any use to other riders.
Only the Mari Lwyd knows they're there.

LIFE IN TEN LINES

Give me a hardback, simple, square and solid.
A paperback's a poor man's substitute
and, by comparison, a little squalid,
which somehow seems to creep in and pollute
a pristine row of standing spines, a mute
concession to a disimproving wrist,
a soft and easy way to get the gist
without the wrestle with the heavy, thick
monstrosity that now defies the fist
and lies, unopened, like a gift-wrapped brick.

HOW BEAUTIFUL ARE THE FEET…
A meditation on the Baptism Altarpiece of
Niccolò di Pietro Gerini (National Gallery)

Jesus is tall. John has to really stretch
so as to tip his terra cotta pot
over the high head of the Son of Man.
God's chuffed. He's just let go the Holy Spirit
to send it plummeting headfirst from heaven.

The kamikaze nosedive showcases
its silly feet, two brown banana skins
that stick out sideways from the fuselage
making me laugh out loud – "Oh, Niccolò,
what a fine thing to offer to the Lord!"

God's good at feet. A whiz at finishing
the legs of birds. I've always loved
the gnarly grabs of irritated chickens,
the whisker-digits of the wren, the soft
underdeveloped token feet of swifts.

I grinned a bit at the lobed toes of coots
until I watched one running on soft mud
with her umbrellas spreading underfoot
to take her safe across the top of it,
turning to oars as she launched on the water.

On the beaches of the Galapagos
the booby shuffles in his blue suede shoes
as though nobody but his love is watching,
despite the shadows of the looming cruisers
and the susurrus of the clicking twitchers.

To each God gave according to its need
regardless of the flocks of jeering hooters.
Lord, may the six feet that I end beneath
lie light as those that have amused me most,
the coot, the booby, and the Holy Ghost.

MAKE YOURSELF AT HOME
Waking in someone else's house…

Always first up, old habits dying hard.
All at my disposal and nothing mine.
Trying to manage the first urgent piss
without a sound. To flush or not to flush?

Last night's dishes are sitting where we left them,
the glasses red-rimmed and apologetic.
Should I wash up? Is there a dishwasher?
What needful things lie behind which closed doors?

Carefully, carefully along the bookshelves
Searching for any signs of a like mind.
Pulling out, putting back, guiltily wondering
whether I might come across one of mine.

Fish out the exercise book and the ballpoint;
let me be caught in the act of creation
when the host enters, my left hand hovering
ready to hide the false starts and the doodles.

Finally, little ploys derived from life;
the calculated accidental nudges
of frequent trips halfway to the bathroom
so as to activate the creaky stair.

At the first indication – *Thar she blows!* –
I sit rehearsing how to fold my face,
readying myself for the inevitable
Good morning! Did you sleep well? Been up long?

ABSOLUTION

Bless me, Cabbie, for I have strayed.
It has been too long since my last visit.
I have been elsewhere and had forgotten
the power and the glory of it.

Exchanging tip for quip, I step, a shriven prodigal,
into the heaving innards, the borborygmus
of my own city.

It is what they expect, the easy knockers,
but their perception is at odds with mine;
the bitter stink of it, the great gurgling roar
wrapping me like a beloved blanket
knitted from muttered multilingual confidences
pierced here and there with sudden dropstitch squeals,
shot through with random strands of lurex laughter.

I pull it round me, hold it with one hand,
turning the gesture into a blessing
by raising the other in a token wave
to the great ongoing process of it,
feeling the welcome back into the fold.

TWO POEMS ABOUT SPAM

Spam 1

Beautiful Spam, so nearly meat,
You came about as a wartime treat
With a pinch of pork and a hint of ham
And a whiff of austerity, beautiful Spam!

Beautiful Spam, who then would wish
For Snoek or any funny fish
Or flesh of billy, bull or ram?
Oh, meat of the multitude, beautiful Spam!

Beautiful Spam, your pale pink prism,
Plonked on a plate with Platonism,
Stands for the grandeur of Uncle Sam.
Gift of America, beautiful Spam!

Beautiful Spam, I thee exalt,
Sodium nitrite, fat and salt,
The fair foundation of all I am.
Feast of obesity, beautiful Spam!

Spam 2

See it slide from the confines of its tin;
it is Milo of Croton, poised and greased
for combat. See the first slice, unwiped, hung
from thumb and finger. Watch it as it slips,
still in its jelly, between eager lips
where its pink dampness will be welcomed in,
held for a moment like a lover's tongue
pressed hard against the palate, then released
to lie, resigned, a sacrifice beneath
the rhythmic strokes of reverential teeth.

NETTLES

Walking with care among armed enemies,
I am harvesting the tips of nettles.
I understand that they are good for me;
vitamins, minerals, trace elements
all wild and free. Nature's contribution
to these uncertain times, where fear and ignorance
combine to make necessity of virtue.

I will blanch them, remove their stringy stalks,
squidge them with scissors, add pinhead oatmeal,
season them well and bind them with an egg
then fry till lightly browned, telling myself
they are close cousins of Pembrokeshire seaweed.
But laverbread, too, is an acquired taste
and frankly not all it's cracked up to be.

MARI LWYD MENDS THE HORSES OF MATHOLWCH

Efnisien took me and broke me.
Not by long-reining, training to bit and saddle,
but blade-hacking me into something less than horse.
My eyes and ears taken, my lips cropped
to wet rags bleeding over my teeth
so that I could not graze for the pain.

I am knocking, knocking.
Let me pass through the door.

Somewhere in a corner of a field
soft with clover, smelling of other than blood,
Nisien waits, shaking a bucket.
I can see him clearly, hear the feed whispering.
I will use my new lips to kiss chaff from his flat palm
and rest my mended head on his honest shoulder.

AND IN WELSH…
(trs. Frank Olding)

Fe gydiodd Efnisien ynof a'm torri.
Nid ag awen hir, na ffrwyn na chyfrwy,
ond â'i lafnwaith erchyll i'm difwyno'n rhywbeth llai na march.
Fy llygaid, fy nghlustiau wedi'u dwyn, fy nghweflau crop
yn garpiau gwlyb yn gwaedu dros fy nannedd
fel na chawn bori rhag y boen.

Rwy'n curo, curo.
Gad imi ddod trwy'r drws.

Rhywle yng nghornel cae
yn feddal gan feillion, ac amgenach sawr na gwaed,
fe erys Nisien, yn ysgwyd bwced.
Fe'i gwelaf yn glir, clywaf sisial gogor.
Defnyddiaf fy ngweflau newydd i gusanu'r eisin o gledr wastad ei law
a phwyso fy mhen trwsiedig ar ei ysgwydd glên.

BONES

Flicking leaf litter with the rubber tip
of any ordinary walking stick
often reveals the skeletal remains
of some small creature that has reached the end
of its allotted span. Here lies a lark
all split and swindled out of its music,
leaving behind a pile of instruments
with which to call it back. Balanced on beads,
a single white maraca sits in silence.
A rib-marimba, underpinned by sinews,
lies alongside a scattering of hammers,
long flutes of legs and a keel-tambourine
to back a gaping beak's absence of singing
in a lament to lay a bird to rest.

ROAD WORKS
*On the dualling of the A465 between
Brymmawr and Abergavenny*

1. Violence in the Clydach Gorge ...

Roadmakers tear the earth with toothy buckets,
turning politely to dollop the gobbets
over their shoulders. Then they bend again
to take the next enthusiastic bite.

> There is glee in the telling of the stories:
> The men whose horse had stopped (perhaps to graze)
> who cut stiff briars to teach a bloody lesson
> not to the horse, but to the poor old woman
> who had passed by and therefore must have cursed
> the creature. Caught her and whipped her till she bled.
> That's what you do to witches. Shakespeare said.

Roadmakers seem to be having a hard job
breaking the old walls that held back the mountain
when everyone assumed the last new road
was going to be as it was forever.

> There is glee in the telling of the stories:
> John Dawson, teacher at the ironworks school,
> strict disciplinarian, had three pets,
> a cat, a jackdaw and a little dog.
> He simply disappeared, but they were found,
> the cat, the jackdaw and the little dog,
> in the pond that he walked past every day.
> Tied up together in a gunnysack.
> His cat. His jackdaw. And his little dog.

Roadmakers tackle a leftover lump,
Lower their cranes to peer helplessly at it
Muster their men to harry it with hammers
Call in the old guard with their whining drills.

2. Up and Over

A stone whose nose lies buried in the dirt
is turned to feel the sunshine on its face
and for a moment, dries and lies inert,
held in a temporary state of grace
until the shadow of the great machine
swings out across the shining sky again
taking great liberties with what has been
to make a topsy-turvy *mise en scène*.
Rocks that for centuries have lain below
spirited suddenly into the light
while others, wind-caressed and lichened, go
below, to lie forever out of sight.
The place anticipates a special guest;
turning the mattress will ensure his rest.

3. Where are they now?

The Drum and Monkey – when did we lose sight of it?
That other good Italian restaurant.
The Little Chef, the pink house to the right of it;
it takes a while to realise they've gone.
The special point of view where the canal
ducked underneath the road, popped out again
and for a moment seemed to run uphill.
The left-hand turn onto the little lane…
There was security in passing them,
ticking them off like moorings on a river.
We travel now from simply missing them
to realising that they've gone forever.
History happens at the moment when
Where are they now? becomes *Where were they then?*

4. A Video of Things to Come

Flying along a road as yet unmade
through countryside not yet as it will be
while the creator of the plan displayed
his vision of the tarmac artery.
Being familiar with an artist's fear
What if? Yes, but… No, no – that isn't it…
I was amazed to see the engineer
claiming a future target as a hit.

In days when men built for a different master
a mason would have been of the same mind,
outthinking every possible disaster,
cherishing what he needs to leave behind.
A green cathedral; rubble, rock and sod
crafted to the greater glory of God.

5. A New Roundabout

Car-Car-Carousel
Round to heaven, round to hell.
Circle-dancing, dangerous play
Who gave you the right of way?
Round, round, here's one more –
This one wasn't here before.
Round, round, one-two-three
Where's the one that used to be?
Round, round, play the game
Each one different, all the same.
Round, round, whoopsy-do,
Find your exit, leave the queue.
If at first you search in vain
Carry on around again.
Round, round, until you find
Where it is you have in mind.
The only one who'll ever tell
Is someone else who's lost as well.

6. Other People's Wheels

A new road is coming to speed the wheels.
Four lanes; two up, two down, will trump the three
where once they dodged each other merrily.
A dotted line used to divide the wheels,
determining which had the middle ground,
and somehow seemed to keep them spinning round.
But that arrangement did not please the wheels;
they wanted unimpeded leave to go
and now the work goes on to make it so.
Meanwhile the lights and cones collect the wheels
in elongated batches, boot to bonnet.
A fine new road, but not much driving on it.
So now they praise the good old days of three
and long to sing the old song - *Poop-poop! Wheee!*

7. Ironing Things

In winter, when the leaves are off the trees,
you get a good view of what's left of it.
Then I, aboard the Stagecoach, scan the hills,
noting the iron-things, the hallowed past
of the land wherein I am a latecomer.

Nominal vaguenesses of "kit" and "gear".
Precarious dram-roads with a *Grande Corniche*
where to-and-fro defeated up-and-down.
Echoes of times when Europe looked this way
to hail the captains of the industry.

The roadmakers, having laundered the gorge,
pummelling the worst stains from the old highway,
spreading green cloth and stitching silver braid,
have found the crumpled bits in hearts and history
and are intent on ironing them out.

There will be bridges, steel but not stainless,
forms that will decorously oxidise
so as to rub the memory of iron
into the healing wound, soon scabbed forever
in a condition of perpetual rust.

I felt that was a rather strange idea
and now, as it becomes reality,
I try to plug my ears against the sound;
a hollow banging on a deadlocked door
and a disheartened whisper – "Nevermore".

CLEARING THE DECKS

1. The Skip

See, I have loaded up the borrowed skip;
its hollow belly has been satisfied.
Now, Haulier, come and take it to the tip
but not before you've spread a net to hide
the sheer enormity of what I've done.
The mighty pile in shameless disarray
teeters like Ossa upon Pelion,
the cruel truth of what I've thrown away.
Not books or tools – both those are sacrosanct -
but so much other once-beloved stuff
that, like an extra tooth, had to be yanked
because it wasn't relevant enough.
To see the back of it should bring relief
and not this synthesis of guilt and grief.

2. The Bonfire

First savour the fugitive whiff of it
sneaking out furtively from the echoing can;
long-ago lamplight, now a chance for change
by way of a little curative mischief.

Burdened with so much arbitrary preciousness
to which I can give no guarantee of forever
I will make it all into one magnificent safety
beyond all argument. I will anneal regret.

Liberally, liberally I have sprinkled the sacrifice
with the scented blessing of the unbreakable promise,
the coming-together of the various to make the last;
the match, the scratch, the flash, the flick, the roar…

STONES WITH SAD FACES

I did not plunder indiscriminately,
it is simply my habit to look down.
I took only those that asked to be taken,
those with appealing eyes that caught my own.
Some had mouths too, and those were a bonus;
a faint approximation of a smile,
a sullen underscore, an aghast O.
Anything that suggested a stone face
booked them a homeward passage in my pocket,
gifts from the places where I first observed them,
mementos that would be forever loved.

I still recall the why of all of them
but most of their wherefroms have petrified
into their now, sideboard and windowsill,
dried-out and dull, accumulating dust.
Muddled and shuffled out of their origins
they call to me, confused, from bowl and basket
till slowly I have come to understand
it would have served them better had I left them
to anonymity among their brethren,
the slow erosion of the elements,
the innocent carelessness of the sea.

THE POND IN JULY.

Summer has taken it and put an end
to Winter's dithering – "Is it time to break,
first the stiff, gripping ice, and then the fast
that holds the goldfish safe against the danger
of sudden frost and undigested food?"

Summer has taken it and made it right;
they are slow-rolling globules in a lava lamp
rising and diving in the limpid juice
that came both slow and sudden to replace
Winter's unappetising muddy gruel.

Summer has taken it. The only thing
that might upset it is the red confetti
from the wedding of overhanging roses
to the erratic breeze, and even these
are soon scooped off, like froth from cappuccino.

Summer has taken it, holding it now
in the safety of long days and hot nights
and all shall be well until the first tap
of Autumn on the shoulder of the year
warns me that soon Winter will want it back.

MARI LWYD AND THE POSTAL PALAVER

Nige made a mini-Mari out of cornstarch,
building her horse-face like a house of cards,
layer by layer on a 3D printer.

He posted her First Class, got a receipt,
let me know she'd be with me the next day.
Then she mysteriously disappeared.

Some jobsworth had jiggled her Large Letter
against the arbitrary cardboard slot
behind the counter, changed it to Small Parcel.

And now the stamp was slightly insufficient.
Mari was sent to the back of the queue
and I received a large ransom demand.

I paid. She came. Ridiculously late,
covered in ignominious stickers
but welcomed and prepared for decoration.

I asked advice. Nige said "acrylic paint
because it sticks like toffee to your jumper".
Two coats were tongue-between-the-teeth applied.

Yacht-varnish settled in a dewy cloud,
fixing her pallor, fixing the stray hair
from the cheap brush forever on her cheek.

I gave her eyes and now they reprimand me
from her place on the corner of the dresser,
making me say "Oh, Mari – why the long face?"

BLACK CAT SINNING

Not hanging offences, any of them,
just irritations, studied and perfected.
Appropriating designated space
and adapting it to her own purpose.
Her wicked sister, on the other hand
(who is never to be seen where she is)
will murder fur-and-feather now and then.
She merely tries to hide the evidence.

There is no backlog to her catalogue
for she attends regularly her place
of convenience and absolution
in her taken-for-granted absences,
returns wide-eyed and joyful. A new cat,
baptised by dew, smelling of flowers in season,
she takes up her position at my elbow
all innocent and free to sin again.

FOMITE
Advice from the British Veterinary Association

All right. I will incarcerate my cat.
I am advised to disinfect her feet
and wipe her fur when she comes back indoors
from any of her clandestine adventures.

Good luck with that! A cat is not a dog
who can be made to relish interference
if it is countered with a compliment
and bought with thirty pieces of liver.

Minimal contact is also advised
with ritual handwashing after each touch.
She is simply a surface after all
and could be easily contaminated.

But kept indoors, hand-smoothed and tongue-shriven,
I need not shrink from contact with her body,
her urgent whispers, languid clawless taps,
her warm weight on my lap like a fuzzy glove.

SYNCHRONICITY

The house honks and a fusty hum appals
my nostrils. While I laboured in the loo,
Cat, in her litter, did the ritual waltz
then squatted down and defecated too.
Our mutual relief is evident
and nothing I can do will stop it stinking.
Cat nonchalantly cleans her fundament.
I sip a cup of tea, sniffing and thinking.
Like typists in a pool, whose monthly flows
will shift until they menstruate together
we two have shat in unison, which shows
how close we have become to one another
and though the smell is bad, the thought is good;
a token of a sort of sisterhood.

PRISONER

I haven't let her out for several days.
At first she cried but now she seems resigned,
uses the litter, eats and sleeps and plays
and yet I can't believe she doesn't mind.
This house is hers, but beyond the locked door
is where she truly lives. I can't do much
to make the trade acceptable to her.
She's dozing by my side, but as I watch
I see her slipping like a twist of silk
through green entanglements, drowsing in sun
on rooftops, watch her haughty high-tailed walk.
I wake at night appalled at what I've done.
I shall I restore her freedom; ban instead
the words that trapped her: Old. Alone. Afraid.

QUARTERSTAFF

High Summer. Striding out just before dawn
along the lowest dram road on the mountain.
Across the valley all the houses lie
like scattered boxes at a birthday party.
If somebody is there, behind a bush
or peeping through a window, what's to see?

Only a stout fellow in a red jerkin
taking a stance, raising a hefty stick
with stretched arms, holding it above his head,
hands clasped equidistant from either end.
Holding the pose awhile, lowering slowly
to pause again, drawing it straight and tight
under his belly, for a count of three.

Will Scarlett, practising in Sherwood Forest
for his next tussle with the Sheriff's men?
No, me, practising breathing – up, and in –
and down, and out. A daily ritual
against the day it may be called upon
to help me hold my ground against a foe.

FENCING

You call across the street, challenging me.
"Oh, there you are. I want to talk to you".
I'm horrified. I know your way of talking,
the edging nearer for the shoulder-touch,
the leaning-in, conspiratorial,
the sudden fingerpoke for emphasis.
These cannot be achieved at a safe distance.
I hide my fear behind a smile. *Allez!*

We stand on the unmarked two-metre *piste*,
prepared to carry out our conversation.
You raise your sabre, open the assault;
I parry, come straight back with a *riposte*.
You move toward me for a *corps-à-corps*,
earning an *avertissement*, "Step back, please."
I effortlessly parry every lunge
till I can call a halt and disengage,
citing the age-old rule of prior engagement,
because I do not choose to be *touchée*.

MISSION IMPOSSIBLE
Cats' Protection: "Neuter and Release"

They are closing in, the grizzled exploiters,
on the silver girl walking the dark street.
She is alone, deferring to her destiny,
their blood is up. Waiting, they wail and bicker.

I, too, am determined to catch her but
she eludes me, more and more preferring
the crude old stagers tempting her with scent
who seek to leave her carrying their shadows.

It is her time, she is almost calling.
See her play the coquette, chasing dry leaves
as the wind rattles them on the tarmac,
a dancing princess soon to be a queen.

I can entice her gently to the threshold
but not yet through the door. She will take food
from proffered fingers, but avoids their grasp
and will not set foot in the careful trap.

Great Pan, lend strength to my conspiracy;
my failure will mean midwinter kittens,
cold, hungry, possibly misbegotten.
Come to me, come, little Mehitabel.

MARI LWYD WITH BELLS AND WHISTLES
Wye Bridge, Chepstow, January 2019

See the army on the bridge, met for battle.
Ramshackle gathering of ghostly horses,
one-off interpretations of a whim.

Once a found skull mounted on a broomstick
bobbing above a man clad in a sack,
going from door to door, a merry beggar.

Now a bedecked, bejewelled artifact
lit from within, giggling with little bells,
pimped like a virgin at a handfasting.

Thirty are gathered, with their entourages,
whose sacks are velvet cloaks; they gloom and glint
as the torches sway in the slow progress.

Not so much cultural appropriation
as new-age sprouting on a found tradition,
mistletoe berries on an ancient tree.

Enthusiasm justifies the theft
and is the reason why the skulls of horses
command high prices on the Internet.

BALLISTIC

It is, as the gardeners say, "going over".
The leaves are disappearing and a few
defiant flowers are clinging, sparse and wet
to the collapsing framework of the plants.

Most of the seed-pods have already burst,
shooting their freight in a mad cannonade.
Their work is done; they have impregnated
their deathbed with another generation.

A few remain, like ten, nine, eight green bottles,
skinny things, hanging sadly on thin wires.
I take them, one by one, into my hand
for my amusement and for their last chance.

Some come at once, spilling their seeds too fast,
a mighty writhing and a lying still,
while others take their time, responding slowly
in a warm palm under a stroking thumb.

Some are beyond my help. I leave those be.
Nature wastes nothing and something will use them.
I have enjoyed the game, and finding out
that some of my old skills still do the trick.

GROWN FROM A STONE

When the first green fist of your cotyledon
burst like a baby from your endosperm
I gave it what it craved to drink and feed on,
foiled the dark love of weevil, thrip and worm.

I kept you on the windowsill at first,
tending you endlessly and smiling smugly
not knowing I'd eventually be cursed
with something so enormous and so ugly.

You're on your seventh pot. You upped your game
when you perceived you had me in your power.
I gave you space to grow, a home, a name;
you've never given me a single flower.

I plan to take you walking after dark,
dig you a shallow grave and set you free.
I'll come and visit you in Pilgrims Park,
my monstrous green responsibility.

NATIVITY PLAY

*Monks come to blows with brooms over who has the
right to clean the Church of the Nativity in Bethlehem*

Down tools, you fools, the Brothers cry,
leave you my church alone!
How dare you white my sepulchre
with your vile holystone?
How dare you cherish what I serve
as if it were your own?

Thus each man kills the thing he loves;
his passion seals its doom.
A tract of land, a stretch of sand,
a rock, a church, a tomb.
Some of them do it with a bomb
and others with a broom.

If Jesus had the casting vote
would any of them care?
But he's long gone, and hasn't left
even an echo there
of how a harlot washed his feet
and wiped them with her hair.

RECLAIMING THE ABANDONED GARDEN

1. Survivors

Coming back to the garden, the dispute resolved,
I found that it hadn't expired, but evolved.
The original concept was more or less whole
but the birch and the bramble had taken control.

The flowers we planted may well still be there
but I can't, at a glance, say undoubtedly where.
The shrubs and the bushes are strong and in leaf
but the birch and the bramble both beggar belief.

The birch is a chancer that leeches thin ground,
the bramble's a monster that reaches around
and clings with its fingers to all vacant spaces
to throttle its rivals and thrive in their places.

These are the trees of backcountry and heath
and the clever food-giver that creeps underneath.
They are the rough, undesirable plants
that colonise habitats nobody wants.

When folk have done thrutching and present is past
and time has decided what's destined to last,
the strongest and fittest will stand up and shout.
The birch and the bramble will see us all out.

2. Hide

The old door whinges as I peer inside.
After a little tussle with the key
I let myself into the wooden hide
you made to aid your ornithology.

Setting aside the struggle with the key,
I find myself alone with what you left
to grease the wheels of ornithology
and I am both delighted and bereft.

I stand alone, looking at what you left -
a book, a glass, a bottle of Sancerre -
I laugh, delighted, and then stop, bereft,
suddenly face to face with who you were.

A book, a glass, a bottle of Sancerre,
a wooden desk, a sketchpad and a pen,
reminding who I am of who you were
and why it was we made the garden then.

I sit down at the desk, take up the pen
and write a memorandum, cut and dried:
I'll mend our garden as we made it then.
The old door chuckles as I step outside.

3. Tench

Pale lips, Ophelia's, kissing the cool surface
before the grey-green turn, the disappearance.
A swift glimpse of an unsuspected tench
left in the depths of the abandoned pond
the day I shut the gate and let it be.

Now, decades later, I've reclaimed the land,
stepping back into the old shared vision,
renewing my acquaintance with the trees,
keeping our promise to the unseen creatures
that have made homes among the dereliction.

I am restoring the neglected pond,
wondering if I'll see those waxy lips,
wishing I might, hoping I don't, believing
that for as long as I remain unsure
the old tench will be safe among the lilies.

Taken for granted, hypothetical,
my faith will save it, like applause for fairies,
like the imagined cat of every colour
preserved forever in a lidless box
as a beloved possibility.

TOAD

I saw the flat stone with a builder's eye.
It had been dumped; nobody wanted it
but I could see a perfect use for it.
I lifted it to test the weight of it
and saw that someone had already claimed it.

A fine old toad was dozing under it
wrinkled and winter-red, pressed like a tongue
into the space it had decided on,
waiting until the sunshine filled its skin
and called it back to action, warts and all.

For weeks I walked that way, seeing the stone,
sometimes allowing myself a quick look
at the unlovely sleeper. I would raise
its flat roof for a moment, set it back
after a blown kiss and a whispered blessing.

At first I thought I must have missed the place
until I realised the stone had gone.
Someone had done what I first meant to do.
There was no trace of the amphibian,
had they killed it or did it crawl away?

If I had claimed it, made it my own toad,
taken it home and given it my garden,
would it be there now, singing in the dark
or would it have been martyred by a car
on the long road back to its lost best place?

UPON A SNAIL
After Bunyan

He goes but slowly but he goeth sure.
His shelly hat nobody doth he doff to.
He leaveth sticky tinsel on the floor
So we can see where he hath slithered off to.
He keeps his innards in a trinket box
As fine as any on a dressing table.
He rolls his eyes up like a pair of socks
And squirts them out again when he is able
To do so without being put upon
By interfering interested parties.
He lives in fear of being trodden on
Or written on by snooty arty-farties.
He eats the food that Nature put for him.
He walks upon his stomach, which is odd,
But Nature made it like a foot for him
And that is why he's called a gastropod.

KIFTSGATE

We are at war now, my ill-chosen rose.
I must tackle the fact that you have cast
your lust for *lebensraum* beyond our borders.
Now with the hee-haw of the pruning saw,
the click of secateurs, the clomp of loppers,
our long alliance ends in confrontation.

I let you have an ash tree of your own
in which you spent your adolescence, climbing
high for the hell of it, building tree-houses
for owls and squirrels, scattering confetti
from lofty pockets, generous with fruit
for any visitors that cared to call.

But that was not enough. You threw yourself
rudely across the intervening spaces
reaching for other trees and farther gardens,
taking long-legged strides in all directions.
Neighbours have noticed. Remarks have been passed
on the unruliness of your behaviour.

In these first skirmishes of our last battle
I face the wasteland of our old encounters.
You have called forces from beyond the grave;
your bramble footsoldiers shackle my ankles
as I contend with your already-dead
whose daggers stab me as I reach for green.

I force my way into your wilderness.
You find unguarded skin above my gloves
lifting it deftly with your wicked fingers
so that I flinch and yelp and tweak it free,
watching it settle slowly back in place
over my old flesh like a wrinkled stocking.

MARI LWYD WILL BE COMING SOON

She is expecting guests. The fine bone china
that belonged to her grandmother, graces
the perfect surface of the immaculate cloth.
All of it out, even the unnecessary;
the extra cruet and the great tureen.

Only a single piece is not in place;
the cup she holds, that lets arthritic fingers
cast youthful shadows through the skin of it
above the amber of the final drop
of stupidly expensive Oolong tea.

She hears them at the door. The tipsy laughter,
clatter of ill-matched lids and dented saucepans.
She puts the cup, unwashed, onto the saucer,
then takes one backward step and, with both hands
she heaves the cloth from underneath the china.

Not a magician's flick. The artless tug
of a first-time destroyer, merely keen
to find out what will happen. All her skills
have hitherto been honed for acquisition
followed by years of care and conservation.

It is as she envisaged. One great fall
of pride and the long crash of desolation.
Outside there is a new silence. Inside
there is the crunch of eggshells underfoot
as she opens the door to the pale horse.

SEAT

The new seat appeared on the next road down
the year my husband died. A brutal thing
made of box section steel, roughly welded,
a metal pallet for bodies in transit.
In winter it assaults the fundament,
sucking the warmth from unsuspecting buttocks,
giving cold comfort to ill-trousered thighs.

We are walking together, she and I,
going down from our terrace past the place
where the cement from when the wall was new
still carries the deep print of my left hand.
As we set off down to the next level,
I take a step backwards, "No, after you."

I stop and watch her going down the steps.
The sun is shining and the seat is warm.
I see her settle on it while she waits
for me to catch her up. She has grown old
little by little in my company.

A breeze ruffles the white hair on her neck.
She settles back and stretches out her arms,
her hands clasped in a benevolent gesture
blessing the bent head of her walking stick.

BADGE OF HONOUR

I have awarded myself the Order of the Staircase.
Pink, round and bouncy, it's a jolly knob
stuck on an ordinary walking stick.

It may look like an old red rubber ball
but, thinking of a thing I should have said
moments after the moment when I didn't,
I turn the stick round, drop it on the floor
so that it bounces back into my hand,
twirl it full circle. Ha! – *Ba-doom Tish*...

I smile, bowing to inaudible applause,
awarding myself another invisible ribbon
to mark the tardy cap-in-hand arrival
of the oh-so-slow *mot juste*.

THE GRAVEDIGGER DIGS THE DIFFERENCE

> *Hamlet: I am but mad north-north-west. When the wind is southerly, I know a hawk from a handsaw.*

So, hawk and handsaw. What's the difference?
Don't listen to the academic fools,
It's only a straightforward reference
To honest artisans and basic tools.
All talk of falconry's misunderstood,
Wrongly subordinating man to master.
A handsaw is a thing for cutting wood,
A hawk's a sort of tray to carry plaster.
A man would automatically heft
A handsaw with a dominant right hand,
Balance a hawk of stucco in his left.
That's all you need to know to understand.
The hawk and handsaw of the working class
Are simply left and right – elbow and arse.

MARI LWYD MEETS MARIE LLOYD.

We are in a theatre. The lights go up – but not very far – as the curtain rises on the outside of a darkened house. A classic child's drawing of a house. A door in the middle with a dimly lit window on either side. A small group is standing by the door; a few undistinguished figures surrounding a Mari Lwyd, who is cowled in a traditional sack over string-gaitered trousers and with somewhat oversized boots. After a bit of shuffling the Mari Lwyd performs the dance song from page one. At the end, one of her entourage raises a stick, gives three portentous knocks on the door and...

The stage revolves to reveal the inside of the house. We see the door and windows from within. A room stacked with boxes. Full lights, spotlight on a "pantomime dame" figure who stands with her back to the audience, hands on hips. She is wearing an elaborate, flounced gown, short enough to reveal buttoned boots, and a huge flowered hat. She turns and is recognisable as Marie Lloyd. The audience cheers.

Marie: Ooh – 'Allo. I must admit I wasn't expecting visitors, so you'll 'ave to excuse the state of the place. We've only just moved in and I 'aven't 'ad time to unpack. I 'aven't even uncovered me cock linnet.

She lifts a covered birdcage, winks, and sings "Don't Dilly Dally on the Way"

At the end of the song the three knocks are heard "again" – they are the same three knocks but now observed from inside.

Marie listens and asks. "Did you 'ear anything?" audience shouts "yes!" At the same time Mari Lwyd appears, looking through the right-hand window. The audience explodes with laughter. Marie turns just as Mari disappears. Marie turns to the audience "Did you see anything?" – "Yes!" "Where?" "At the window!" Marie turns and takes a few steps towards the right-hand window. Mari appears in the left-hand window and the audience laughs again.

Classic Panto banter. "Tell me if you see anything"- audience shouts when Mari appears; Marie keeps missing it. "What did you see?" "A Horse!" Again Marie misses the window appearance, turns to the audience – "An 'orse? An 'orse? – My kingdom fer a bloomin' 'orse…" She turns her back to the audience, strides to the door, flings it open and Mari Lwyd stands framed in it.

The audience applauds. Marie, hands on hips, appraises the newcomer, then turns and ushers Mari inside. "I don't know who you are, but one look at those teeth tells me we must be related". The audience roars – Marie's teeth are legendary.

Mari enters, cautiously. As the scene progresses, Marie dresses Mari in bizarre clothes – one of the window curtains, an antimacassar, the tasselled cover from the linnet's cage. Marie sings "A little of what you fancy" and they share a clog-dance routine. At the end of the duet they embrace.

Curtain

The stage revolves again and we are outside once more.

Curtain Call. Marie and Mari come out of the door, walk to the footlights and take the burst of applause. Marie is bareheaded, grey-haired and walking with a stick. Mari is now wearing Marie's hat. They are both transformed.